La Fayette Grover, John F. Miller, John E. Ross, Martin V Brown

Report of Governor Grover to General Schofield on the Modoc War

La Fayette Grover, John F. Miller, John E. Ross, Martin V Brown

Report of Governor Grover to General Schofield on the Modoc War

ISBN/EAN: 9783744710527

Printed in Europe, USA, Canada, Australia, Japan

Cover: Foto ©ninafisch / pixelio.de

More available books at **www.hansebooks.com**

REPORT

OF

GOVERNOR GROVER

TO

GENERAL SCHOFIELD

ON THE

MODOC WAR,

AND

REPORTS OF MAJ. GEN. JOHN F. MILLER AND
GENERAL JOHN E. ROSS,

TO THE GOVERNOR.

ALSO LETTER OF THE GOVERNOR TO THE SECRETARY OF THE INTERIOR
ON THE WALLOWA VALLEY INDIAN QUESTION.

SALEM, OREGON:
MART. V. BROWN, STATE PRINTER.
1874.

E99
.M707
x

GOVERNOR GROVER'S LETTER

TO

GEN. SCHOFIELD

ON THE

MODOC WAR.

To Major General J. M. Schofield,
  Commanding Military Division of the Pacific:

Sir—In reply to your communication of June 4, 1873, in which you request that I will cause a muster roll of the forces called out by me to be properly certified to, and forwarded to your headquarters, and also to state if those troops were called out at the invitation or solicitation, or by the authority of any military officer of the United States, and if any such officer, by any act or promise has in any manner committed the United States to liability for transportation, forage, subsistence, clothing, equipage, etc., said information being desired on account of the death of General Canby and the removal of officers on his personal staff:

I have the honor to communicate the following: In the initiation of the late Modoc service no direct requisition was made by General Canby, then in command of the

Department of the Columbia, on the authorities of the State of Oregon, for troops, but there was a recognized co-operation by the Oregon Volunteer Militia in the field with the regular troops, and the volunteers served during their first campaign against the Modocs, under the command of the military officers of the United States, in the field, with the approval of General Canby.

The circumstances attending the calling out of the Oregon Volunteers appeared at the time to be imperative to meet a sudden emergency. In order to exhibit clearly the nature and necessity of this service it will be proper to detail some of the leading facts antecedent to actual hostilities. The Modoc tribe of Indians have been known since the earliest immigration to Oregon and Northern California as a band of murderers and robbers. They have earned the character of being the most treacherous and blood-thirsty savages west of the Rocky Mountains. They occupied a country peculiarly adapted to protect them in their practice of slaughter and to shield them from successful pursuit and capture. Innocent and unoffending emigrants, with their wives and families, passing through the Modoc country along the old southern overland road to Oregon, have been attacked and butchered indiscriminately by these fiends, their property taken or destroyed and their bodies inhumanly mutilated and left unburied a prey to wolves. In some cases their victims were made to suffer the pains of the most cruel tortures before relieved by death, and in some cases girls have been kept among them as captives for months to suffer more than torture, and in the end to meet their miserable death.

Over three hundred emigrants are known to have been slain in this manner by these Indians, ascertained by actual count of their bleaching bones upon the soil, before the establishment of the military post at Fort Klamath, in 1863. This post was established for the protection of the immigrant trail and to make an end to the slaughter and rapine of which these savages were constantly guilty. In 1864 a treaty was made with the Indians in the Klamath Lake Basin, including the Modocs, by which they ceded all their lands to the United States, except those included in the Klamath Reservation, and agreed to reside exclusively upon said Reservation. In the mean time the public lands in that vicinity had been surveyed under the authority of the Surveyor General of Oregon, and the same were opened for settlement. The Modocs went upon the Klamath Reservation, according to the stipulations of the treaty, but not to remain. They soon went back to their former haunts, alleging dissatisfaction with their treatment at the hands of the United States Indian Agent. They made their homes at different points to suit their convenience and their roving dispositions. The country having now become partially occupied by settlers under the preemption acts of Congress, these Indians began a system of petty annoyances to the settlers with the evident intention of inducing them to abandon their settlements. They would visit houses in the absence of the male members of the family and demand that the women should, at unreasonable hours, cook food for their parties, which they generally did, at great hardship and expense, for the sake of peace. The Modocs claimed the ownership of all the lands which they had sold, and demanded of the settlers rents, for occupancy, and compensation for cutting grass, grazing, etc., which demands were complied with for the purpose of preserving peace. This conduct caused many settlers to leave their claims, and with their families leave the country. But the settlers who remained, generally maintained friendly relations with the Modocs, notwithstanding their bad conduct and unlawful presence and exactions.

The Superintendent of Indian Affairs for Oregon made frequent, but unsuccessful, attempts to induce these Indians by peaceable means to go upon their Reservation. In the month of November, 1872, the Superintendent having personally conferred with the Indian Department, at Washington, proceeded to Link river, in the Klamath country, for the purpose of requiring the Modocs to comply with the stipulations of the treaty. At this time the Modocs were camped in three separate bands as follows: Capt. Jack, with several warriors and their families about three miles from the mouth of Lost river, on the west side; Hooker Jim, a petty chief, with his band, occupied the shore of Tule Lake, east of the mouth of Lost river, in Oregon; the Hot Creek band were camped on the south side of Little Klamath Lake, in California, some twenty-five miles from Capt. Jack's band, in a southwesterly direction.

On the 27th day of November, 1872, the Superintendent having failed, by peaceable means to induce Captain Jack to assent to a return to the reservation, addressed a letter to the officer in command at Fort Klamath, stating that the Modoc Indians defiantly declined to meet him according to his request, and declared that they would not go upon the Reservation, and made the following requisition: "In order, therefore, to carry out instructions from the Commissioner of Indian Affairs, I have to request that you at once furnish a sufficient force to compel said Indians to go to Camp Yainax, on said Reservation, where I have made provision for their subsistence." [See enclosure "A."]

Previous to this time, upon being advised by the Superintendent that he had been instructed to put these Indians upon the Reservation, Gen. Canby placed all the military force and material of the United States in that section of country under the control of the senior officer of that district, Lieut. Col. Frank Wheaton, 21st U. S. Infantry, for the purpose of effecting the removal of the Modocs by force, if need be; at the same time indicating that the time and manner of the removal had not been determined, but that he should be prepared for the possibility that the attempt to remove them might result in hostilities, and that he should, in that event, act promptly for the protection of the frontier. The force specially designated to this duty consisted of four companies of cavalry and three of infantry, distributed among the garrisons at Fort Klamath, Camp Warner and Camp Harney, in Oregon, and Camp Bidwell, in California, [See inclosure "B," letter of General Canby to Governor of Oregon.] None of these posts were within immediate supporting distance to Fort Klamath, and the force at the latter post was entirely inadequate to the duty contemplated.

At this point two very incomprehensible and disastrous circumstances occurred.

1st, The order of the Indian Department for the removal of the Modocs by force was not delivered to the officer specially designated by Gen. Canby for that duty; and,

2d, No notice whatever was given to the neighboring settlers that difficulties were pending.

The result was that on the 29th day of November, 1872, a small detachment of troops, thirty-five men, under command of Captain James Jackson, approached Captain Jack's camp, early in the morning, and demanded that he surrender and go upon the reservation, according to the terms of the treaty. This was refused, and upon further demand the troops were fired upon by the Indians. Upon this first fire one citizen, happening to be present, and who was not aware of the circumstances, was killed. During, and subsequent to the affair between the command of Capt. Jackson and the band on the west side of Lost river, under Capt. Jack, the Indians under Hooker Jim, on the shore of Tule Lake, east of the mouth of Lost river, scattered in small parties among the isolated settlements for twenty-five miles around and massacred eighteen unoffending and unsuspecting citizens and sacked and destroyed their residences, and drove off their cattle and horses. This work of butchery and pillage lasted for two days. Eleven citizens were murdered on the 29th and seven on the 30th of November, by the savages under the lead of Hooker Jim. This band had not been approached by the soldiery. Capt. Jack's band, after the fight, fled south on the west side of Tule Lake to the Lava Beds, along the rocky ridges not inhabited, and therefore committed no murder in their flight. The Hot Creek band, on the south side of Little Klamath, took no part in the massacre of settlers, but appeared to be friendly and expressed a willingness to go upon the Reservation. Immediately after the massacre steps were taken to have this band return to the Reservation, but owing to the great and natural excitement in the country it was thought best by Gen. Canby to have protection for these Indians.

In the meantime dismay spread throughout the settlements of Southern Oregon, and a demand was made by the people upon the Governor for troops to protect the living and bury the dead. A Volunteer company of citizens was raised immediately; public meetings were held, and urgent calls upon the Governor for orders authorizing the recognition of their services. Temporary orders were given with direction to act in conjunction with the regular troops. [See inclosure "C."]

On the 2d of December the Governor received a telegram from the Superintendent of Indian Affairs at Jacksonville that assistance was needed at Klamath, that the citizens were without arms, and requesting the forwarding of one hundred latest improved muskets. [See inclosure "D."]

At this time there had been no concentration of troops to the point of disturbance, and there was no available force of United States troops ready for immediate action in the Klamath Lake Basin. Col. John E. Ross, of Jackson county, was by telegram appointed Brigadier General of the First Brigade of Oregon Militia, and instructed to do all that was proper in the emergency, but to see to it that when sufficient force of United States troops should reach the field, to withdraw the Volunteers. [See inclosure "E."] Gen. Ross promptly accepted the commission and entered upon his duty.

A letter was despatched to Maj. Gen. E. R. S. Canby commanding this department, informing him of these circumstances, and soliciting instant action on the part of the regular forces. [See inclosure "F."] Gen. Canby responded, sending copies of his orders, directing all available force in the district to be placed in the field to protect the settlements and to chastise the savages. The Hot Creek band of Modocs, numbering about forty, men, women and children, on the 6th of December, had not yet joined the hostiles, and being not implicated in the murders which had been committed were expected to arrive at Yreka, California, to be transported to the Klamath Reservation via Rogue River Valley, Oregon, and owing

2M

to the excited condition of the country a force was requested by Gen. Canby for their escort. Having no disposable force himself he made requisition on the Governor of Oregon for assistance, at the same time stating that the band under Capt. Jack, and all those implicated in the murder of citizens, would be captured and crushed out, and all the murderers would be turned over to the civil authorities for trial and punishment.

The policy affecting the murderers of the citizens had been agreed upon by the Governor and Gen. Canby in a personal interview. In response to this requisition Gen. Ross was ordered to use his authority and influence to place the peaceable Hot Creek's on the Reservation, but on the night of the 5th of December, after the wagons and teams had been prepared for their transportation to the Reservation, by way of Yreka and Rogue River Valley, and after having promised to go peaceably, the whole band stole away in the night time and fled to the Lava Beds to join Capt. Jack, and from that time worked and fought with him throughout the war. [See inclosure "G."]

Gen. Ross' force was small—two companies—Company A, Capt. Harrison Kelly, and Company B, Capt. Oliver C. Applegate. He arrived in the Klamath Lake Basin on the 9th of December. At this time no United States troops had arrived at the scene of the late massacre. Gen. Ross' first work was to place his men in position to cut off communication between the hostiles and the reservation Indians, then to dispatch a force to seek for survivors of the Lost river settlement, and to bury the dead, whose bodies had now lain exposed to beasts of prey, without sepulture, for ten days.

This sad duty performed, he proceeded, according to instructions, to offer his services in co-operation with the regular troops who had now begun to arrive in the vicinity of the Lava Beds, from the several distant posts in the District. The United States officer in command received Gen. Ross cordially and issued an order for his co-operation. [See inclosure "H," Gen. Ross' Report, and Orders of U. S. officer.] -

The field of operations being crossed by the boundary line between Oregon and California, and the hostile Indians having taken refuge in the pedrigal situated wholly in California, General Ross' services, from this period, during his first campaign against the Modocs, were entirely within the State of California, for the purpose of dislodging an enemy infesting our borders, but acting under orders of officers of the Army of the United States.

The volunteer services on the part of the State of Oregon were intended to meet a pressing emergency in the absence of regular troops. On the 16th of December, therefore, the Governor issued an order to General Ross to muster the volunteers out of service in case a force of United States troops sufficient for the protection of the southern frontier had taken the field. But he was instructed to use his discretion as to whether the emergency of the case required the further presence of the State troops. [See inclosure "I."]

On the arrival of Lieut. Col. Frank Wheaton, the officer in command of the District of the Lakes, he fully approved the action of Major John Green in inviting the co-operation of the Oregon Militia, and in his General Field Order No. 1, assigned General Ross to duty as a part of the force designated to make the main attack upon Captain Jack's stronghold in the Lava Rocks. [See inclosure "J."]

This order contemplated the delay of several days for preparation for the attack. The Oregon Volunteers having been mustered for a sudden emergency only, and being without tents, and without a sufficient supply of blankets and rations for further service, and being too far distant from their base of supplies for being supplied in these particulars by the State, these facts were made known to Col. Wheaton. This officer immediately gave orders for the issue to Gen. Ross' command such blankets and other supplies as he had at command, for the immediate relief of the Volunteers, with the understanding that they should continue in the field until the concerted attack upon the Modocs. This arrangement was acted upon. [See inclosure "K."]

Before receiving the reports of General Ross as to the concerted movement upon the Modocs, and being uncertain of the condition of the settlements, and of the Volunteer service, by order of the Governor of January 7, 1873, Major General John F. Miller, of the Oregon Militia, was directed to make a visit of observation to the southern frontier, to distribute arms among the settlers and to muster the Volunteers out of service on ascertaining that regular troops had occupied the field in sufficient force to protect the settlements and chastise the savages. Gen. Miller found the Volunteers in hearty co-operation with the regular troops, and that Col. Wheaton desired them to remain in the field under his orders until after the pending attack, which was confidently expected to be final. Gen. Miller coincided with the views of Col. Wheaton, and remained himself, and took an active part in the battle of the Lava Beds of the 17th of January. [See inclosure "L," Gen. Miller's Report.]

The issue of Quartermaster and Commissary stores to the Volunteers were duly reported by Col. Wheaton to Gen. Canby, and by him approved; and the same were finally approved by the decision of the Secretary of War, in the following words; "As it appears that the issues to the Oregon Volunteer Militia, made by order of Col. Wheaton, were sanctioned by Gen. Canby, and were necessary to prevent the men from suffering when cordially co-operaating with the United States troops, while under the exigencies of the service their numbers were inadequate for the protection of the settlements against Indian attacks, the Secretary of War approves the action of Col. Wheaton." [See inclosure "M," a certified copy of said decision.]

On the 17th of January the first general engagement was fought with the Modocs. This battle was well contested under the circumstances; and though not successful, it clearly exposed the difficulties of the field and the character of the enemy.

General Canby having ordered out all the available regular force in Oregon and California to reinforce Col. Wheaton, and having informed the Governor that he had no doubt that he would be able to protect the frontier and subdue the Modocs, the Volunteers were withdrawn from the field and were mustered out of service as expeditiously as possible. [See inclosure "N."]

During this expedition the Oregon Volunteers not only served under the command of regular officers of the United States, but they were detailed to perform escort duty in regular transportation, and their teams and wagons being light and serviceable in a muddy region, were used in connection with regular army transportation to good advantage. In fact, there was a blending of the Volunteers with the regular force.

SECOND EXPEDITION OF THE OREGON MILITIA.

The second service of the Oregon Volunteer Militia,

composed of Company C., Captain Joseph H. Hyzer, Company D., Captain Thomas Mulholland, and Company E., Captain George R. Rodgers, was called into reqisition in the month of April, after a period of very unsettled feeling, growing out of doubts in the minds of all frontier settlers as to the results of pending negotiations for peace with the Modoc savages, without first subduing them, or demanding the surrender of the perpetrators of the massacre of the 29th and 30th of November. When these negotiations were abruptly terminated by the double perfidy of the savages, and the assassination of Gen. Canby and Commissioner Thomas, the whole country exposed to the raids of the Modocs, became excited with the dread of more massacres. The regular forces which had been concentrated near the Lava Beds were not disposed by the new commander, Col. Gillem, with any reference to giving protection to the Oregon frontier. All the available regular force in the Department of the Columbia had been ordered to the support of Col. Gillem, so that there was not, at the time of calling these companies into service, a single company of regular troops in the State of Oregon, while its eastern and southern settlements were exposed to the dangers of a general Indian outbreak. Gen. Ross, in his report of the second Volunteer service remarks upon this point as follows: "Let us now pause for a moment and consider the condition of the settlements of Southeastern Oregon. The massacre of the Peace Commissioners was, of course, the signal for the renewal of Indian hostilities. If the Modocs should fall back from the Lava Beds, the settlements referred to would be at the mercy of the Indians. Or, if the Indians on the Klamath Reservation, who had thus far remained friendly, should determine to join the hostiles, of which there was great danger, their first movement would be to murder the settlers, burn their houses and drive off their stock. It will thus be seen that the southeastern portion of the State was in constant and imminent peril; for upon the happening of either or both the contingencies referred to, the settlements in that section would fall an easy prey to Indian cruelty and rapacity. Under these circumstances an adequate military force in the Lake Basin, to prevent by their presence an outbreak on the part of the Indians on the Reservation, and also to protect the settlements from the hostile Modocs, became an indispensable necessity." [See inclosure "O," Gen. Ross' report of second service.]

The first applications on the part of the people for a second call for troops were denied by the Governor, but becoming satisfied that the Klamath Reservation Indians were no longer trustworthy, and that the peril demanding action was imminent, a call was made.

The massacre of the Peace Commissioners occurred on the 11th day of April, 1873, and Col. Gillem immediately commenced an attack upon the Indians in the Lava Beds. The engagement lasted three days, resulting in routing the savages from their first stronghold, only to have them fall back to another, which gave them access to the Lost River country, and the Klamath region, and exposed all the settlements of Southeastern Oregon to their raids. At this time the Indians on the Klamath Reservation, who had been armed by authority of the agent, were threatening an outbreak. Col. Gillem sent out couriers to warn settlers and to stop communications, except by way of Yreka, California. Other Indians were making demonstrations of hostility. It now appeared that a general Indian war of serious magnitude could only be prevented by throwing a force of Volunteers into the field north of the

California line, to intercept communication between the Modocs and the Klamath Reservation, and with the Snake and Piute Indians. The three companies already mentioned were authorized by the Governor and directed to open the road from Jacksonville to the Lake Basin, and to go at once to the relief of the endangered settlers. [See inclosure "P."]

On learning that a force of Volunteers had been ordered to the Klamath country, the U. S. Indian Agent at the Klamath Agency, L. S. Dyar, addressed a letter to Gen. Ross in which he said: "I respectfully request that you send a strong detachment to Yainax, (on the Klamath Reservation.) Such a course would, I think, not only protect the settlers on Upper Sprague River, but would do more to prevent a general outbreak than anything else perhaps that you could do, as it would almost insure quiet among the Snakes and Modocs now there, and prevent a raid upon that place by Captain Jack. A successful raid upon Yainax would nearly double Captian Jack's warriors. Will you not represent this matter to Governor Grover." [Inclosure "Q."]

There being no regular troops in Oregon at this time, there was great apprehension of an outbreak of the armed Reservation Indians, and of a general hostile uprising of the neighboring tribes of the southern border. The condition of the settlers of the Lake Basin was now considered most critical. The hostile Modocs on one side and the threatening Reservation Indians upon the other, so impressed the settlers with the danger of their situation that they were abandoning their homes, removing their stock and property and fleeing out of the country. [See inclosure "R."]

The Indian Agent removed his family from the Klamath Reservation and left the place himself. The air was filled with dangerous rumors, and the most discreet and temperate men considered general hostilties imminent. A false step at this juncture would have precipitated a general outbreak. The arrival of the Volunteers, therefore, appeared to be a most opportune relief. As to disarming the Indians on the reservation the Governor's instructions to Gen. Ross were: "Great care must be taken upon this question, not to move prematurely for disarming any Indians by indiscreet action, or by such movements as will excite hostilities that cannot be controlled by the force present. The policy is to arm the settlers, and by a small and active force to assist in their defence until the United States can furnish troops for that purpose." [See inclosure "P."]

Gen. Ross moved with caution and discretion. [See inclosure S.]

He dispatched Company D, for the protection of the settlers of Drew's Valley, and the Valleys of Goose Lake, Chewaucan and Summer Lake, these being in great danger from raiding parties of Captain Jack's Indians, who were now scattering from the Lava Beds.

Companies E and C were stationed at different points in the settlements, west of those above named, and were employed in scouting the country so as to make their presence and their object known both to the friendly and to the hostile Indians. In the meantime, on the 2d of May, Gen. Jefferson C. Davis, having been assigned to the command of the Department of the Columbia, arrived at the Lava Beds and took personal command of the U. S. forces operating against the Modocs. Shortly after this vigorous movements against Captain Jack were apparent, and a successful onslaught was made by the

3M

regulars upon his camp on Sorass Lake, on the 10th of May, with the U. S. forces operating in his front, with the Oregon Militia cutting off his communication with the Reservation Indians, the Piutes and the Snakes, and finally, with disaffection in his own ranks, his desperate alternative was fight or surrender. The closing events of the Volunteer service are thus reported by Gen. Ross:

"Learning on the morning of the 26th of May that Captain Jack, with a portion of his warriors, had made their escape from the Lava Beds, and gone in the direction of Langell Valley, I started immediately with Capt. Hyzer's Company, accompanied by my staff, and arrived at the eastern end of the valley referred to on the evening of the 31st. Soon after going into camp a scouting party was sent out with orders to examine the ground for sign of the fugitive Modocs, and after a short absence the party returned, reporting the discovery of fresh Indian tracks on the mountain south of our camp. Thereupon I immediately dispatched 1st Lieut. Lindsay, of Company C, with twenty picked men to occupy the summit of the mountain referred to, with orders to keep a sharp watch for Indians, to capture all he discovered, and to shoot down all that refused to surrender. Meanwhile having learned that Maj. John Green, U. S. A., with his command was camped some four miles east of me, I dispatched a courier to him next morning to inform him of my whereabouts and of the discovery made on the evening previous. In a short time Maj. Green came to my camp, and expressed a desire that my troops act in concert with those of the United States in capturing the fugitive Modocs. A party of those Indians were believed to be in the vicinity of a small lake in the mountains, ten miles south of our camp A plan of co-operation for the capture of these Indians was agreed upon between Maj. Green and myself, in pursuance of which both commands moved by different routes at midnight, on the 1st of June, for the point referred to. My troops being the first to arrive at the place designated, and discovering fresh Indian tracks, started immediately in pursuit and followed the trail until night coming on they were compelled to camp. As soon as day dawned next morning the pursuit was resumed and kept up all day over an extremely rough country. At dark the Indians were overtaken and captured. The captives numbered 12, among whom was the notorious 'Black Jim,' one of the murderers of Gen. Canby.

"Next day, June 4th, I sent a message to Gen. Green, informing him of the captures we had made, and also forwarded a dispatch to your Excellency upon the same subject. In reply I received a note from Maj. Green, requesting me to send my captives to an island in Tule Lake, at which all the Indian prisoners were being collected. (See copy of his letter hereunto attached.) I also received a telegram from your Excellency, containing instructions in regard to the same subject. In obedience to these orders I took immediate steps to ascertain if any of these Indians stood indicted in the Circuit Court of Jackson County, for the murder of the Lost River settlers, and having become satisfied that none of them were concerned in that massacre, I proceeded with my captives to the island referred to, and delivered them up to the commanding officer of the U. S. troops at that place."

The Modoc war now being brought to a successful termination by the capture of Captain Jack, and the principal portion of his warriors, and there being no further necessity for any troops in the field, I issued a general order that they proceed at once to the respective places at which they were enrolled and be mustered out of service.

Accompanying herewith I transmit six muster rolls, numbered from one to six inclusive, being as follows:

1st, Muster Roll of General Field and Staff Officers.
2d, Muster Roll of Company "A."
3d,   "   "   "B."
4th,   "   "   "C."
5th,   "   "   "D."
6th,   "   "   "E."

I also transmit herewith an "abstract of indebtedness of State of Oregon on account of expenses of Modoc war of 1872-3."

FIRST SERVICE.

Also "abstract of indebtedness of State of Oregon, on account of expenses of suppressing Indian hostilities," etc.

MODOC WAR—SECOND SERVICE.

Amounting respectively to the sums of........$ 60,826 55½
                                              69,901 88½

Amounting in the aggregate to...........$130,728 44

Col. Jesse Baker, Quartermaster General, and Col. J. N. T. Miller, Commissary General, gave their personal attention to much of the duties pertaining to their several departments. Maj. Quincy A. Brooks, Assistant Quartermaster General has had personal supervision of closing the accounts. I believe that the service has been conducted with prudence and integrity. Col. Miller was with the Volunteer troops throughout the first service, and has furnished me with many important facts relating to he same. Copies of subordinate abstracts, returns and vouchers, will be furnished upon request.

Very respectfully,
Your obedient servant,
L. F. GROVER,
Governor of Oregon.

STATE OF OREGON, EXECUTIVE OFFICE, }
Salem, February 13, 1874.

REPORT

OF

MAJOR GENERAL JOHN F. MILLER

TO

GOVERNOR GROVER.

HEADQUARTERS DISTRICT OF THE LAKES,
And of the U. S. Troops and Oregon
Volunteer Militia operating in the
Modoc country.
Cam,, near Van Bremen Ranch,
January 20, 1873.

To his Excellency, L. F. Grover, Governor of Oregon:

SIR—I have the honor to report that, in conformity with the General Field Order No. 3, issued by Brevet Major General Frank Wheaton, U. S. A., Commanding District of the Lakes, a copy of which is herewith enclosed, the Modoc position was attacked early on the morning of the 17th inst., by the Oregon Volunteer Militia, under Brigadier General J. E. Ross. Two companies, " A," Captain Harrison Kelly, and " B," Captain O. C. Applegate, each numbering some sixty men, including twenty Indian scouts belonging to company " B," and an independent company of California volunteers, twenty-five in number (Captain John A. Fairchilds), co-operating with about two hundred and fifty troops of the United States under Brevet Major General Frank Wheaton, U. S. A. The engagement begun at 8:30 A. M., and continued until dark, and, owing to the position of the enemy, which it was impossible to forsee or provide against, resulted in the discomfiture of our attacking forces, with a loss of about forty men in killed and wounded, including two killed of the Oregon Volunteers.

The Oregon Volunteer Militia, under General Ross, in order to accomplish the most effective service, have, since the commencement of operations against the Modocs, placed themselves under the direction and command of General Wheaton, an officer of great ability and experience.

From the most reliable information at my command I estimate the number of hostile Indians at not less than one hundred and fifty warriors, and, from information derived from scouting parties and others, and which I deem reliable, many of their females fight with a desperation and courage equal to that of the males.

Their position is in what is known as the "Lava Bed," an immense plain of volcanic rock, cut and broken with fissures, canyons and chasms, on the south of Tule Lake, about ten miles south of the boundary line between Oregon and California. It is one of great strength, and difficult of approach. It is the opinion of General Wheaton, and Majors Green and Mason, that it will require one thousand men, with mortars and provisions for a siege of perhaps many days, to dislodge and capture them; and, from my own observation, I concur in their opinion.

The home of these Indians is in Oregon. The scene of their depredations is along the border of either of the States of Oregon and California, and their victims are the defenseless citizens of both States. Settlers, not longer since than last summer, have been terrified by insults to their families, and the fear of massacre, into removing from the country, while others have been compelled to procure temporary immunity by giving them certificates of good character and gratuities of food. One settler, Henry Miller, was massacred by them within a few months after having given such a certificate. They must be conquered and removed to distant Reservations, or the country here abandoned to them. I am satisfied that no force, that it would be practicable to place upon our frontier, could entirely protect it from their raids, and the withdrawal of the force now here would invite them to renewed robberies and massacre.

The term of enlistment, of the Oregon Volunteers now here, has, with a few exceptions, expired, and, within a few days, they will be mustered out of service.

General Wheaton, if supported by the proper authority, will put an end to Indian troubles in this vicinity for all future time. He has gained information, by the movement of the 17th inst., of the position of these Indians that is indispensable to successful operations against them, and that could only be obtained by a reconnoisance in force. His coolness and excellent judgment in the affair of the "Lava Beds" were conspicuous throughout. The same honorable mention is due to Majors John Green and E. C. Mason, both, like General Wheaton, veterans of the late war, and the former a man of large experience in Indian fighting with General Crook, Colonels David Perry and R. F. Bernard, Captains J. Q. Adams, G. H. Burton and James Jackson, Lieutenants Ross, Rheem and Moore of the 21st Infantry, and Lieutenants Boutelle and Kyle of the 1st Cavalry. Colonel Perry and Lieutenant Kyle are painfully wounded. Surgeon McElderry, of Fort Klamath, and Acting Assistant Surgeons Skinner, White and Durrant, were under fire during the entire day, rendering prompt service to the wounded of both regular and volunteer forces. The management of the volunteers by General Ross and his subordinates, Captains Kelly, Applegate and J. R. Neil, the latter of General Ross' Staff, was admirable. Captain E. D. Foudray, also of General Ross' Staff, accompanied his Commander upon the field. Hon. J. N. T. Miller was present, and rendered important service during the engagement. At General Ross' request he has been actively engaged in the field from the commencement of hostilities. The volunteers conducted themselves in the most creditable manner, and in a manner honorable to the State. Surgeon Bell, of the volunteers, was promptly at his post in the field.

The Independent Company of California Volunteers, Captain John A. Fairchilds, occupied a most important position on the extreme left, and were greatly exposed during the entire day. They formed a portion of the party under Major Green and Colonel Perry, that forced its way over great natural obstacles, and through a most terrible fire, to a junction with Captain Bernard's forces on the east. Four (4) of this Company were seriously wounded.

The courtesy of the officers of the United States Army commanding here, toward the volunteers, has been marked and uniform, and their material assistance to our troops has been valuable.

General Wheaton moved his headquarters and temporary field depot to this point, where a concentration of the forces was made for the attack. On the 23d inst. his headquarters and field depot will be re-established in Lost

River Valley, near Tule Lake, in Oregon, a much more central and controlling point. The volunteer headquarters will, about the same time, be established at some point in that vicinity.

I have assigned Colonel William Thompson, of the Governor's Staff (by order transferred to service with me), and Colonel C. B. Bellinger, to duty in the field. They accompanied me, and participated in the engagement of the 17th inst.

Mr. Ivan Applegate was present upon the field during the engagement, and rendered important service.

Very respectfully and
Obediently yours,
JOHN F. MILLER,
Major General O. S. M.

REPORT
OF
GENERAL JOHN E. ROSS
TO
HIS EXCELLENCY GOVERNOR GROVER.

                        HEADQUARTERS 1ST BRIGADE
                          OREGON MOUNTED MILITIA,
                        Jacksonville, February 20, 1873.

His Excellency
    L. F. Grover, Governor of Oregon,
                                    Salem, Oregon:

SIR:—I have the honor to submit the following report of the operations of the troops under my command in their recent campaign against the Modoc Indians.

Before doing so, however, permit me to submit a few remarks in reference to the origin of the Modoc war.

An order had been made by the Secretary of the Interior, that the Modoc Indians, then encamped on Lost River, should return immediately to their (the Klamath) Reservation. The Indians refused to obey. Maj. James Jackson, U. S. A., with 35 men, was directed to carry the order into execution. This force being entirely too small to command obedience, the Indians at once commenced hostilities, by butchering the settlers on Lost River, who were entirely ignorant of any impending conflict between the tribe and the Government. It should be remembered also, that these murders were not committed whilst actual war was raging between the Indians and the United States, but that they were perpetrated before that state of affairs had an existence. The U. S. troops were on the west side of Lost River, as was also the camp of Captain Jack, the head chief of the Modocs. The settlers that were massacred, lived and were murdered on the east side of that river. The Messenger of the Superintendent of Indian Affairs went to the Indians camped on the east side of the river and notified them that they were required to go immediately upon the Reservation. Whilst the proper officers were urging the Indians to go upon the Reservation, they (the Indians) commenced firing, and the first person killed was John Thurber, a private citizen. This was on Friday, November 29th, 1872. A number of the other settlers soon met a similar fate, and the survivors fled for refuge to the house of Dennis Crawley, pursued by the Indians. Meanwhile two other citizens, W. Nus and Joseph Penwig, ignorant of what was going on, were riding up toward Crawley's house; the Indians rode out and met them, saluted them in a friendly manner but suddenly fired upon them, killing Nus instantly and severely wounding Penwig, who succeeded, however, in making his escape. In all, eighteen inoffensive settlers were thus inhumanly butchered. Meanwhile, the Indians having fired upon the troops, the fire was returned, but Maj. Jackson's command being entirely inadequate to cope with the savages, was forced to retire. Such was the origin of the Modoc war; a war commenced on the part of the Indians by an unprovoked and cold blooded massacre of inoffensive settlers, butchered whilst pursuing their usual avocations, and who met their terrible fate, not during the existence of a state of recognized warfare, but immediately anterior to its commencement, i. e. in time of peace.

In obedience to your Excellency's instructions, I enlisted two companies of Mounted Militia, whose term of service commenced on the 2d of December last. By the 7th of that month most of my command was mounted and equipped, and sent forward to the settlers in the Klamath Lake Basin, and on that date, after detailing Maj. W. A. Owen of my staff, to act as Quartermaster and Commissary for the Brigade, with instructions to make his headquarters at Jacksonville, and to purchase and forward with dispatch all necessary supplies for the troops, I started for the front accompanied by my two Aids-de-Camp, Capts. E. D. Foudray and J. R. Niel, and also Col. J. N. T. Miller, Commissary General. Maj. J. N. Bell, the Brigade Surgeon, had started the day previous. We arrived at Linkville on the 9th.

The two companies referred to consisted of Co. A, Capt. H. Kelly, and Co. B., Capt. O. C. Applegate. Capt. Kelly had temporarily established his headquarters at the north end of Tule Lake, some ten miles from the mouth of Lost River, and was engaged in searching for the bodies of the settlers that had recently been murdered by the Indians. Capt. Applegate was directed to station a part of his company at Yainax, on the Klamath Indian Reservation, until further orders, to protect the United States property there; to scout over the surrounding valley; to guard the settlers from being raided upon by Indians, and to cut off all communication between the hostile Modocs and friendly Modocs on the Reservation. The remainder of Co. B, under 1st Lieut. J. H. Hyzer, accompanied my headquarters.

On the 10th December I arrived at Capt. Kelly's camp and the following day his men succeeded in finding the last of the missing bodies of the murdered settlers, which I forwarded to Linkville for burial. There being now no further need of a military force in the vicinity of Lost River, the settlers having all fled the country or been murdered by the Indians, I determined to move my troops to a position on the west side of Tule Lake, as near as practicable to Captain Jack's stronghold in the Lava Beds, and on the morning of the 12th we started for the point referred to. On our way we passed the camp of Maj. John Green, U. S. A., to whom I communicated your Excellency's instructions to co-operate with the U. S. forces in the field. Maj. Green was much pleased to receive this information, cordially approved any proposed change of position, and promised to send Capt. David Perry with Co. F, 1st Cavalry, to join me in a couple of days. We arrived at Van Bremer's ranch on Willow Creek, California, the same evening after a hard day's march of 40 miles. We found the ranch deserted and a notice on the door to the effect that the proprietor had fled through fear of Indians.

Next day Capt. John A. Fairchild's, the owner of a ranch in the vicinity, and who afterwards, as Captain of a Company of California Volunteers, co-operated with us against the Modocs, came to my headquarters, stated that himself and neighbors, being entirely unprotected, were in constant danger of being killed by the Indians, and expressed himself as highly pleased that we had come to their relief. I informed him that we were Oregon Militia, and being then in the State of California, we were beyond our proper limits and would have to return to our own State, unless the officer in command of the U. S. forces ordered otherwise.

The above facts I also communicated to Maj. Green, then in command of the U. S. troops, operating in that section, who immediately issued Field Order No. 2, ordering me to station my troops at such points as I might "deem best for the protection of the people in the State of California against the raids of the Modoc Indians." [See the order hereto attached.]

In the evening of December 13th I was joined by Capt. D. Perry, U. S. A., and his command. On the 15th, Capt. Kelly, Co. A., with twenty-five men, First Lieut. J. H. Hyzer, Co. B, with ten men, Capt. J. R. Neil, of my staff, and Capt. Perry, U. S. A., with thirty men, made the first reconnoissance of the Indian strongholds in the Lava Beds.

It being now deemed best by Capt. Perry and myself, for the protection of the settlements northwest of Little Klamath Lake, that my troops should take a position in that locality, I moved my command on the 19th of December, and established my headquarters at Small's ranch, on the Klamath River. The condition of the road across the mountains being such as to make it impossible for teams to transport supplies as fast as needed, I next day, in company with Capt. Foudray, of my staff, made a visit to Linkville to secure some additional stores for my troops.

Whilst at Linkville it was my good fortune to meet and form the acquaintance of Major General Frank Wheaton, U. S. A., Commander of the District of the Lakes, who had just arrived and was gratified to learn that your Excellency had instructed me to act in concert with the U. S. forces operating against the Modoc Indians. He also assured me that the presence of our Volunteer Militia in the field was actually necessary, and on learning that we were needing some more blankets he gave an order on the quartermaster at Fort Klamath for an adequate supply,

5M

stating at the same time that anything he could do to make my troops comfortable would be cheerfully done.

Returning from Linkville I reached Small's ranch in the evening of the 21st of December, and immediately issued to my troops the supplies I had procured.

Next morning, in company with Col. Miller and Capt. Neil, I left headquarters with the view of selecting a camp near the Indian stronghold. While at the house of P. A. Dorris a courier reached me, direct from Captain Perry, informing me that the command of Col. R. F. Bernard, U. S. A., had been attacked by the Indians in full force, on the south side of Tule Lake; that he (Capt. Perry) had gone to Bernard's relief, and requesting me to push forward my troops without delay to his assistance. A courier was dispatched at once, with orders to Capt. Kelly and Lieut. Hyzer to come up immediately, which orders were promptly executed, and upon the arrival of the troops they were sent forward to Captain Perry's relief. About ten miles beyond Van Bremer's, however, our troops met Captain Perry and his command returning, the Indians who attacked Bernard having been driven back. In consequence of this attack Captain Perry deemed it best that my headquarters should be re-established at Van Bremer's, to which I assented, and this move was effected in the night of the 22d of December.

On the 5th of January Captain Kelly, Co. A., with ten of his men, accompanied by Donald McKay, and four friendly Indians, under orders from me to view out a shorter route between Van Bremer's and the Lava Bed, came upon and attacked a party of 18 or 20 Modocs. The Indians fled to the outer edge of the Lava Beds, not far from the Modoc camp, and gave battle from behind rocks. Captain Kelly fought them until Captain Jack and his band coming up and being about to surround our men,

Captain Kelly fell back and offered battle on the open ground. This offer, however, although Jack's force greatly outnumbered ours, was declined, and the enemy retiring to their stronghold, Captain Kelly and his men returned to camp.

On the 9th of January, in obedience to the order of Gen. Wheaton (See his Special Field Order, No. 8, hereto attached), I stationed Co. A, Captain Kelly, on Cottonwood Creek, about eight miles from Van Bremer's, at the intersection of the Modoc trail with the main road, for the purpose of escorting supplies; to guard the Whittle's Ferry road against interruption by hostile Indians, as also to afford more adequate protection to the citizens located southwest of Little Klamath Lake.

On the 12th of January Capt. Applegate and his company, accompanied by Col. Miller, of the Oregon Militia, with Captain Perry, U. S. A., and 13 men, the whole under the command of Major Green, U. S. A., had a lively brush with the enemy, at the top of the bluff overlooking the Lava Bed, in which the Modocs were forced to retire beyond the range of our guns. It is not known certainly what damage was inflicted on the Indians in this engagement, as their warriors were carried off as fast as hurt, but it is believed they suffered the loss of four or five men, whilst our troops were uninjured.

On the same day Maj. Gen. John F. Miller, of the Oregon Militia, with his staff officers, Col. C. B. Bellinger and Cal. Wm. Thompson, arrived at my headquarters.

The 16th January was the day fixed by Maj. Gen. Wheaton, (see his General Field Orders, Nos. 1 and 3, herewith attached) for an advance movement of the Regular and Volunteer forces, under his command, with a view of making a combined attack the next day, the 17th, on Captain Jack's stronghold. The line of battle was to be formed as follows: Capt. Fairchilds, with his company of California Volunteer Rifles, was to hold the extreme left, resting his left flank on Tule Lake; Col. Mason's forces to be on Fairchild's right; Capt. Kelly's company on Mason's right; Capt. Applegate's company on Kelly's right and Capt. Perry's command on Applegate's right, with Lieut. Ross, U. S. A. and twenty men, in the rear to guard the Howitzer Battery. Col. Bernard, with his forces and those of Maj. Jackson on the east side of the Lake, was to form into line of battle with his right resting on Tule Lake, and advancing simultaneously to form a connection with Capt. Perry's right, so as to enclose the southern side of the Modoc position. The immediate command of the entire force operating against the Modocs was given to Maj. John Green, U. S. A., to whom was entrusted the execution of the general plan of operations, as also the details of the attack. Our united forces were as follows: U. S. forces, about 310; Oregon Militia, 115; California Volunteers, 25. Total, 450.

On the morning of the 16th January I moved my command in the direction of the bluff overlooking the Lava Bed, for a position some three miles west of Captain Jack's camp, reaching the desired point in the afternoon where we encamped for the night. Capt. Perry, having started earlier, had taken possession of the bluff and driven off the Indian scouts or pickets. Col. Bernard had also moved out from the east side of the Lake, but getting into an engagement with the enemy was compelled to fall back.

On the 17th January, at 4 o'clock in the morning, my entire command marched down the bluff and took position in line of battle as designated in the Field Orders referred to.

When all was ready and the command given the line moved forward, our advance being directly into the so-called "Lava Beds." The ground traversed was covered at intervals with irregular masses of volcanic rock, whilst a dense fog prevailed over the entire region. These impediments, it is true, made our advance somewhat laborious and difficult, but in no wise dampened the ardor of the troops. After proceeding a mile and a half the enemy opened fire upon us, the first volley being fired in front of Capt. Kelly's company. Soon the firing of the enemy extended along our entire front and was promptly and vigorously returned. But the Indians being secreted behind rocks and crags, in caves and deep fissures, our bullets, though well aimed, had little or no effect. When charged upon in one rock fortress the enemy would retire to another position equally formidable. The difficulties of our advance, owing to these natural obstructions, and the fact that we were constantly exposed to the raking fire of a concealed enemy, were now greatly increased. Moreover, the Indians were perfectly familiar with every crag, crevice and chasm in this immense lava field, whilst our knowledge, in respect to these particulars, amounted practically to nothing. About 11 o'clock A. M. Capt. Perry, in obedience to the order of Maj. Green, changed the position of his company from Capt. Applegate's right to the right of Maj. Mason and connecting with Capt. Kelly's left. The dense fog of the morning had not yet lifted; still our line moved steadily on, driving the Indians before us, but there seemed to be no end to the rocky strongholds to which they could fall back. Our successful charges and the noble enthusiasm of the troops, were therefore of little avail. Meanwhile, we were suffering severely in killed and wounded, without being able to inflict any very serious injury upon the enemy. About 3 P. M. our troops on the west side of the lake were ordered to form a connection with those of Col. Bernard, on the east side, by a flank movement to the left.

The necessity for this order was owing to the fact that the disaster met with by Col. Bernard on the day previous, rendered it impossible for him to form a connection with our extreme right, as stated in the general orders referred to. Meanwhile, the unequal contest in which all the advantages were against us, was kept up with undiminished vigor.

About 5 o'clock P. M., whilst engaged in the flank movement referred to, it was discovered that Major Green, who had the immediate command of the troops, as before stated, together with Col. Mason and Captain Perry, with their respective commands, had been cut off by the Indians from the main line and from all communication with General Wheaton's headquarters.

At this juncture, Gen. Wheaton, in view of the situation, and the absence of Major Green, deemed it proper to give me the immediate command of the remaining forces in the field, using also these words: "Gen. Ross, I now leave this matter with you."

I hastened at once to act in the capacity indicated. We had been enveloped in fog all day, and the Indian war whoop and roar of guns had been kept up without intermission. Our troops had fought for nine hours with heroic bravery, and had suffered a loss of forty men, killed and wounded, but without gaining any important advantage over the enemy; night was upon us; the weather was extremely cold and our overcoats and blankets had been left behind at camp. Moreover, if the Indians with their superior knowledge of the ground, should make a night attack on us we might suffer considerable additional loss. Under these circumstances I determined, with the assent of my superior officers, to move the troops back to our camp of the preceding night, leaving the enemy in possession of the field and our dead. With as little delay as possible therefore, we gathered up our wounded and got our troops in motion; Company B, Capt. Applegate, being in front and Co. A, Capt. Kelly, acting as rear guard, and reached our camp back on the bluff about 10 o'clock that night.

Next morning we ascertained that Major Green, as also Col. Mason, Capt. Perry, Col. Bernard and Maj. Jackson, with their respective commands, had withdrawn during the night previous to Col. Bernard's camp on the east side of the lake.

Gen. Wheaton now decided, after consultation with Gen. Miller, myself and other officers, that a further attack upon the Indians in the Lava Bed was not advisable.

The casualties of the previous day may be briefly summed up as follows, viz: U. S. troops, 37 killed and wounded; Oregon Militia, 2 killed and 5 slightly wounded; California Volunteers, 4 wounded, of whom 2 afterwards died. The two members of the Oregon Militia, who lost their lives in this engagement, were privates John R. Brown, Co. A, and William F. Trimble, Co. B, both brave men, who fell while gallantly discharging their duty.

The actual strength of the enemy in this engagement is not known, but is estimated at from 150 to 200, all well armed, together with quite a number of squaws, who are known to have rendered service as warriors.

On the morning after the battle, and before moving from our camp on the bluffs, in compliance with the view of General Wheaton, as also for the purpose of affording better protection to the settlements, I issued orders making the following disposition of the troops under my command, viz: Capt. Applegate with a portion of Co. B to be stationed at Yainax; Lieut. Hyzer, with a portion of Co. B, to be stationed at Schneider's Ferry; the remainder of Co. B to be stationed at Langell's Valley; Lieut. Reams, with a portion of Co. A, to be stationed at the ranch of Capt. Fairchilds, and the remainder of Co. A, together with myself and staff, to remain at the headquarters of Gen. Wheaton, until the return of the commands that had been cut off from us on the day previous. Pursuant to these arrangements, the troops started at once for their several destinations, and in company with General Wheaton I arrived at Van Bremer's on the afternoon of the 18th of January.

Maj. Green, as also the commands of Col. Mason and Capt. Perry, having all reached Gen. Wheaton's headquarters by the 22d January, on the morning of the 23d I marched with Co. A to Schneider's Ferry. Next day, January 24th, the term of enlistment of my men having expired, and U. S. troops having arrived to take the place of my own, in the protection of the settlement, I issued my General Field Order No. 3, for the disbandment of the 1st Brigade Oregon Mounted Militia.

For a more specific and detailed account of the movements and services performed by Companies A and B of my command, you are respectfully referred to the reports of Captains Kelly and Applegate, hereunto attached.

In conclusion, permit me to say, in reference to the troops under my command, that the field of their operations was in a region of country whose altitude was some 4,500 feet above the level of the ocean, distant from the

Rogue River Valley, my base of supplies, some 80 miles, and separated from that valley by a high range of mountains; that the period of our service was during midwinter, at which season the road over the mountains referred to was at all times exceedingly difficult for loaded teams to travel, and much of the time utterly impassable; that in the hurry with which the troops were sent into the field, some necessary articles were unavoidably omitted, and that the supplies forwarded by Maj. Owen from Jacksonville did not always, owing to the impassable condition of the road, reach us as soon as needed; that my command performed a vast amount of hard marching, and endured at times much suffering from the severity of the weather, necessarily incident to the high altitude of the country and the inclement season of the year. But my troops always responded with promptness to every demand made upon their patriotism, enduring every hardship patiently, and evincing under the most adverse circumstances, a devotion to duty that would have done credit to veteran soldiers.

I desire to state that the gallantry and bravery displayed in the engagement of the 17th by Gen. Wheaton, Maj. Green, Col. Mason, and Captains Perry, Adams and Burton, is worthy of highest commendation; and that their gentlemanly courtesy to myself and staff, as also the generous provision made by the Commanding Officer, for the comfort of my troops, will ever be gratefully remembered.

I will also add that the company of California Riflemen, commanded by Capt. John A. Fairchilds, bore themselves nobly, displaying a dauntless courage and bravery, alike creditable to themselves and the State in whose service they were enlisted.

6M

I desire to state also that Maj. Gen. Miller and his two staff officers, Col's. Bellinger and Thompson, as also Col. Miller, Com. Gen'l., occupied positions in the line of battle, and by their brave conduct, proved themselves worthy of the commissions they hold under the broad seal of the State of Oregon.

I have the honor to be, sir,
Very respectfully,
Your obd't serv't,
JOHN E. ROSS.
Brig. Gen'l. 1st Brig Ogn. Mil.

HEADQUARTERS, 1ST BRIGADE,
OREGON STATE MILITIA,
Jacksonville, Oregon, July 4, 1873.

To His Excellency L. F. Grover, Governor of Oregon, Salem, Oregon:

SIR :—I have the honor to submit the following report of the operations of the First Brigade of Oregon Mounted Militia, being their second service, in the late Modoc war.

As this force was called into service by your Excellency, at the request of the people, for the purpose of suppressing Indian hostilities, and protecting the settlements in the eastern portion of Jackson county, it may not be improper to give a brief statement of the facts which made the presence of these troops necessary in the field.

After the battle of the Lava Beds, on the 17th of January last, a Peace Commission was appointed by the President to negotiate terms of peace with the Modoc Indians. Hopes were entertained that this Commission would be able to so adjust all matters of difficulty with those Indians, as to secure a permanent peace with the tribe. During the progress of the negotiations, however, it became apparent that no faith whatever was to be placed in any peaceful professions of the Indians, and members of the Board, becoming satisfied, from time to time, of this state of affairs, would resign. But their places were promptly filled by the appointment of new Commissioners, it being strongly desired by the General Government that the Modoc difficulties should be settled by treaty without further bloodshed.

In this way negotiations were kept up for about three months, when the proceedings of the Board were brought to an abrupt termination by an attempt on the part of the Indians to massacre the entire Commission. This attempt was partially successful, Gen. Canby and Rev. Mr. Thomas being killed on the spot, Mr. Meacham, another of the Commissioners being badly wounded and left for dead, and L. S. Dyar, the remaining Commissioner, only saving his life by flight. This terrible act of perfidy and savage cruelty of course put an end to peaceful negotiations, and the Indians, recuperated by this three months' rest, reinforced by renegades from other tribes, and strengthened by additional supplies of arms, ammunition, clothing and subsistence, which they had all this time been collecting, again started on the war path, with increased vigor and ferocity.

At this time, it should be borne in mind, that all the U. S. troops heretofore stationed in Southeastern Oregon had been removed south of our State boundary line, leaving the settlements of the Lake Basin without any military force whatever to protect them. In fact there was not at this time a single company of U. S. troops within the limits of the State of Oregon. Let us now pause for a moment to consider the condition of the settlements of Southeastern Oregon. The massacre of the Peace Commissioners was, of course, the signal for the renewal of Indian hostilities. If the Modocs should fall back upon the Lava Beds, the settlements referred to would be at the mercy of the Indians. Or, if the Indians on the Klamath Reservation, who had thus far remained friendly, should determine to join the hostiles—of which there was great danger—their first movement would be to murder the settlers, burn their houses and drive off their stock. It will thus be seen that the southeastern portion of the State was in constant and imminent peril, for upon the happening of either or both the contingencies referred to, the settlements in that section would fall an easy prey to Indian cruelty and rapacity.

Under these circumstances an adequate military force in the Lake Basin, to prevent by their presence an outbreak on the part of the Indians on the Reservation, and also to protect the settlements from hostile Modocs, became an indispensable necessity. But there being no U. S. troops for this purpose, the only alternative left was to raise the required force by a volunteer enrollment of the Oregon Militia. Still your Excellency, anxious to avoid expense, and hoping that the U. S. troops would soon terminate the war, declined at first to authorize the enrollment of any State troops.

The massacre of the Peace Commissioners occurred April 11, 1873. Gen. Gillem, then in command of the U. S. forces in the field, immediately commenced an attack upon the Indians in the Lava Beds. The fighting lasted three days, at the expiration of which time, the Indians, having been cut off from water, although not defeated.

withdrew from their first position in the Lava Beds and retired to another. It was understood by this movement, that the Indians had abandoned the Lava Beds entirely and fallen back into the Lost river country, for the purpose of raiding upon settlements, cutting off communication with the Lake Basin and forcing the Indians on the Klamath Reservation to join them. By order of Gen. Gillem, couriers were dispatched to warn the settlers of their danger, and stop communication with that country, except by way of Yreka, California. The U. S. troops in their three days fight had accomplished nothing towards improving the situation of affairs. In fact the settlements of southeastern Oregon were more than ever at the mercy of infuriated savages. Moreover the Chief Winnemucca, with his band of Piutes, and the Chief Ocheho, with his band of Snakes, had been making war demonstrations, and it was now apparent that a general Indian outbreak could only be prevented, if at all, by throwing a force of Volunteers into the field north of the California line. Under these circumstances, your Excellency was again earnestly besought by our citizens to authorize enlistment of Militia, and this time their petition was granted.

In compliance with your instructions of the 14th of April, I proceeded at once to enroll three companies of Mounted Militia, to be mustered into the 1st Brigade. These troops, when raised, consisted of Company C, Capt. H. Hyzer; Company D, Capt. Thomas Mulholland, and Company E, Capt. George R. Rogers. The men were equipped as rapidly as possible, and sent forward in detachments into the Lake Basin, my object being to keep the road open between that section and the Rogue River Valley, to protect the settlements from raids of the Modocs, and to prevent by our presence in the field, the

Indians who had thus far remained friendly from joining the hostiles. In order to secure a speedy termination of the war, as much depended upon my ability to prevent any further outbreak of Indians, as upon the success of the U. S. troops, now operating against the Modocs in the Lava Beds south of the Oregon line.

About this time I received a letter from L. S. Dyar, Esq., U. S. Indian Agent in charge of the Klamath Indian Reservation, from which I make the following extract: "I respectfully request that you send a strong detachment to Yainax—a station on the Klamath Reservation. Such a course would, I think, not only protect the settlers upon the Upper Sprague River, but would do more to prevent a general Indian outbreak than anything else that you could do, as it would almost insure quiet among the Snakes and Modocs now there, and prevent a raid upon that place by Capt. Jack's warriors." Being satisfied that the views of Agent Dyar, as above expressed, were correct, an adequate force of Militia was stationed at the point above referred to, in compliance with his request.

The settlers in Drews Valley, as also in the valleys of Goose Lake, Chewaucan and Summer Lake, being in great danger of being raided upon by the Indians, Capt. Mulholland was ordered to proceed with his company to those valleys as rapidly as possible, and station his force so as to afford the greatest protection in his power to those settlements.

Companies C and E were stationed at different points in the settlements, west of those above named, and were employed in scouting the country, so as to make their presence and their object known to both the friendly and hostile Indians. Meanwhile the United States troops were operating vigorously against Capt. Jack and his band of murderers in the Lava Beds, and I now felt certain that the objects for which my troops had been raised would be accomplished, and that the war would soon be brought to a speedy and successful termination.

The disaster met with by the Indians in their attack near Sorass Lake, on the 10th of May, proved to be the turning point in the campaign, and the position of Capt. Jack, after that, became hopeless. With the United States forces operating in his front, with disaffection in his own camp, and with the Oregon Militia cutting off all hope of assistance from the Indians on the Reservation, he had no other alternative than to surrender.

Learning on the morning of the 26th of May that Capt. Jack, with a portion of his warriors, had made their escape from the Lava Beds and gone in the direction of Langell Valley, I started immediately with Capt. Hyzer's Company, accompanied by my staff, and arrived at the eastern end of the valley referred to on the evening of the 31st. Soon after going into camp, a scouting party was sent out with orders to examine the ground for signs of the fugitive Modocs, and after a short absence the party returned reporting the discovery of fresh Indian tracks on a mountain south of our camp. Thereupon I immediately dispatched 1st Lieut. Lindsay, of Company C, with twenty picked men to occupy the summit of the mountain referred to with orders to keep a sharp watch for Indians, to capture all he discovered, and to shoot down all that refused to surrender. Meanwhile having learned that Major John Green, U. S. A., with his command, was camped some four miles east of me, I dispatched a courier to him next morning to inform him of my whereabouts, and of the discovery made on the evening previous. In a short time Major Green came to my camp, and expressed a desire that my troops act in concert with those of the United States in capturing the fugitive Modocs. A party of those Indians were believed to be in the vicinity of a small lake in the mountains ten miles east of our camp. A plan of co-operation for the capture of those Indians was agreed upon between Major Green and myself, in pursuance of which both commands moved by different routes at midnight, on the first of June, for the point referred to. My troops being the first to arrive at the place designated, and discovering fresh Indian tracks, started immediately in pursuit and followed the trail until night coming on they were compelled to camp. As soon as day dawned next morning the pursuit was renewed and kept up all day over an extremely rough country. At dark the Indians were overtaken and captured. The captives numbered twelve, among whom was the notorious "Black Jim," one of the murderers of Gen. Canby.

Next day, June 4th, I sent a messenger to Major Green, informing him of the captures we had made, and also forwarded a dispatch to your Excellency upon the same subject. In reply I received a note from Major Green, requesting me to send my captives to an island in Tule Lake, at which all the Indian captives were being collected. [See copy of his letter hereunto attached.] I also received a telegram from your Excellency containing instructions in regard to the same subject. In obedience to these orders I took immediate steps to ascertain if any of these Indians stood indicted in the Circuit Court of Jackson county for the murder of the Lost river settlers, and having become satisfied that none of them were concerned in that massacre, I proceeded with my captives to the island referred to and delivered them up to the commanding officer of the U. S. troops at that place.

The Modoc war being now brought to a successful termination by the capture of Capt. Jack and the principal portion of his warriors, and there being no further necessity for my troops in the field, I issued a general order that they proceed at once to the respective places at which they were enrolled and be mustered out of the service.

In conclusion I desire to state that much credit is due to our Militia for the prompt and energetic manner in which they discharged their duty; and that they successfully accomplished all the objects for which they were enrolled.

    Very respectfully,
     Your obedient servant,
      JOHN E. ROSS,
      Brig. Gen. 1st Brig., O. M.

REPORTS TO GEN'L ROSS.

HEADQUARTERS IN THE FIELD, }
Crawley's Ranch, December 14, 1872. }

Field Order No. 2.

Brigadier General John E. Ross, 1st Brigade Oregon Militia, with his volunteer force, will station his troops at such points as he may deem best for the protection of the people in the State of California against the raids of the Modoc Indians.

JOHN GREEN,
Major 1st U S. Cavalry, Commanding.

WILLOW CREEK, 2 o'clock, A. M.

GENERAL ROSS—Enclosed you will find communication from Major Green, which explains itself. I shall leave immediately by trail for the "Lava Beds," and would like your support in case I should be driven back. My wagons, with a small guard, are on the road, and, if possible, I would like to have you secure them as well as the rancher at this place.

I am, General, very respectfully,

D. PERRY,
Captain 1st U. S. Cavalry.

HEADQUARTERS DISTRICT OF THE LAKES,
And of the Troops operating in the
Modoc country.
Camp near Crawley's Ranch,
Lost River, Oregon, Dec. 20, 1872.

General Field Order No. 1.

I. The disposition of the troops, and all field orders and instructions heretofore given by Major John Green, 1st Cavalry, are fully approved.

II. Major John Green, 1st Cavalry, will retain the immediate command of the troops now acting under his orders, and attack the Modoc Indians wherever, in his opinion, sufficient supplies and ammunition are received, as it is reported, by parties who are familiar with Modoc Jack's location, that it is inaccessible to mounted troops, and that three miles of skirmishing on foot will be required before reaching the Modoc position.

Major Green will not make the attack until the troops are well provided with ammunition. Each man should be furnished with one hundred and fifty (150) rounds, sixty (60) on his person, and the remainder in close reserve, if that amount can be procured.

III. From information thus far obtained it is deemed best to make the strongest attack on the west side of the Modoc position and Tule Lake. The battalion, 21st Infantry, Companies "C" and "B," sixty-four (64) rifled muskets, under Major E. C. Mason; Captain D. Perry, Troop "F," 1st Cavalry, fifty (50) sabres; Major James Jakson, Troop "B," 1st Cavalry, thirty-five (35) sabres; and General John E. Ross, Oregon Volunteers, supposed to number about fifty (50) rifles, will make the main attack. Captain R. F. Bernard, Troop "G," 1st Cavalry, with a detachment of Klamath scouts, the number to be designated by Major Green, will co-operate with the main attack, moving simultaneously on the Modoc position, and on the east side from his present camp near Land's ranch.

IV. Major Green will cause frequent reconnoisances from the several commands, to be made while prepartions for the final attack are being made, and report anything of interest to the District Commander, who will remain in the field with or near the troops until further operations against the Modocs are unnecessary.

It may become necessary to change or modify this general plan of operations, and Major Green will be advised from time to time of any proposed change.

V. If, during or after the attack on the Modocs, they should escape from their rocks and caves, Major Green will promptly pursue with all the mounted force, and kill or capture every hostile Modoc of Captain Jack's murdering band, unless they unconditionally surrender.

VI. If rapid pursuit becomes necessary, Major E. C. Mason's battalion, 21st Infantry, will be left near the Modoc camp, where he will receive orders from the District Commander.

VII. A temporary field depot of supplies is hereby established at this camp. Lieutenant W. H. Boyle, 21st Infantry (acting Adjutant, and A. A. Q. M. and A. C. S. of the 21st Infantry battalion), will, in addition to his other duties, receive and issue supplies on properly approved requisitions. Lieutenant Boyle will communicate at once with Lieutenant Robert Pollock, 21st Infantry A. A. Q. M., at Fort Klamath, Oregon, the officer responsible for supplies sent here, and keep him fully advised of the issues and reception of stores for troops in the field.

When Major Mason's battalion moves, Lieutenant W. H. Boyle will, until further orders from Headquarters,

District of the Lakes, remain in charge of the camp and supplies near Crawley's ranch.

VIII. All reports, returns, etc., will be made to or through these Headquarters, and requisitions for supplies forwarded for the action of the Commanding Officer, District of the Lakes.

By order of

FRANK WHEATON,
Brevet Major General U. S. A., Lieut. Col. 21st Infantry, Commanding District of the Lakes.

OFFICIAL—
JNO. Q. ADAMS,
First Lieut. 1st Cavalry, A. A. A. General.

HEADQUARTERS DISTRICT OF THE LAKES,
And of Troops operating in the Modoc country.
Camp near Van Bremer's,
Willow Creek, California,
January 9, 1873.

Special Field Order No. 8.

With a view to the more adequate protection of the citizens located southwest of Little Klamath Lake, and to guard against the interruption of hostile Modocs on the Whittle's Ferry Road, General Ross, Oregon Militia, will detail, from the two companies now with him in the field, such a force as he may deem necessary, and encamp them at the most advantageous point.

A force encamped near Dorris' Ranch would be able to

escort supplies, and, at the same time, be advisable if a sudden movement from this camp should be ordered.

By order of
FRANK WHEATON,
Brevet Major General, U. S. A., Lieut. Col. 21st Infantry, Commanding District of the Lakes.

OFFICIAL—

JNO. Q. ADAMS,
First Lieut., 1st Cavalry, A. A. A. General.

HEADQUARTERS DISTRICT OF THE LAKES,
And of the Troops operating in the Modoc country.
Camp near Van Bremer's,
California, January 12, 1873,

General Field Order No. 3.

I. The troops will move from their present camps east and west of the Lava Beds, on Thursday the 16th of January, and take positions for the attack on the Modoc camp at sunrise on the following morning.

II. At four A. M., on Thursday next, Major John Green will detach Captain D. Perry's Troop "F," 1st Cavalry, and order it to clear the bluff southwest of Tule Lake of Indian pickets and scouts, and cover the movement of the main force to a camp some three miles west of the Modoc position.

III. Major E. C. Mason's battalion, 21st Infantry, (two companies), "C," Captain G. H. Burton; and "B," commanded by 2d Lieutenant H. D. W. Moore, and a detachment of twenty (20) men of Company "F," 21st Infantry, under 1st Sergeant John McNamara; General John E. Ross, Oregon Volunteer Militia (two companies): "A,"

Captain H. Kelly, and "B," Captain O. C. Applegate, and Lieutenant W. H. Miller's Battery (a section of mountain howitzers), will march from Van Bremer's Ranch to camp on bluff, west of Tule Lake, in time to reach the designated camp not later than three P. M. on the 16th instant. The camp will be so located and arranged as to be secure from observation by the Modocs, and every precaution taken to prevent the Indians from discovering our numbers and precise location.

IV. District headquarters will accompany the troops.

V. Early on the 17th of January the troops above named will move into the Lava Beds to attack the Modoc camp, and in the following order: Major E. C. Mason's battalion, 21st Infantry leading, followed by General John E. Ross, Oregon Volunteer Militia, (the section of howitzers packed). Captain D. Perry, troop "F," 1st Cavalry, will follow the Howitzer Battery.

VI. When the troops have reached a position near the Modoc camp the main force will be deployed on the right of the infantry battalion in close skirmish order, and a left half-wheel of the whole line will be executed, in order to enclose the southern side of the Modoc position and connect the right of the main force with the left of Captain Bernard's troops, who are simultaneously to attack on the east.

VII. All the troops operating against the Modocs are to move from their camps with three day's cooked rations in haversacks, two blankets, one hundred (100) rounds of ammunition on the person, and fifty (50) rounds in close reserve. Canteens will be filled at Little Klamath Lake by the troops from Van Bremer's Ranch, and care taken to water every horse and pack mule at that point, as there is no water on the bluff where the main force will encamp on the night of the 16th.

VIII. Major John Green, 1st Cavalry, is charged with the execution of these movements and the details of the attack.

IX. Lieut. W. H. Miller, 1st Cavalry, commanding the Howitzer Battery, will report to Major Green for orders and instructions as to when and where to prepare his guns for action in the proposed attack.

X. The troops on the east side of the Lava Beds, at Land's Ranch, Cos. "G," Capt. R. F. Bernard, and "B," Captain James Jackson, 1st Cavalry, and the Klamath Indian scouts, under Dave Hill, will move from camp on the 16th inst., to a point not more than two (2) miles from the Modoc position. At sunrise on the 17th this force will attack the Modoc camp with their right resting on or near Tule Lake, and when sufficiently near to render the movement advisable, a right half-wheel will be executed in order to connect the left of this force with the troops attacking from the west. In his advance Captain Bernard will take steps to capture any canoes the Modocs may have near their camp, or at least use every effort to prevent Indians from escaping by water. Captain R. F. Bernard, 1st Cavalry, will execute these movements under such detailed instructions as he may receive from Major John Green, 1st Cavalry.

XI. After the first three (3) shots have been fired from the Howitzer Battery, as a signal to the troops attacking on the east side of the Modoc camp, firing will cease for fifteen (15) minutes, and an Indian scout directed to notify the nearest Modocs that ten (10) minutes time will be allowed them to permit their women and children to come into our lines. Any proposition by the Modocs to surrender will be referred at once to the District Commander, who will be present.

XII. Lieut. W. H. Boyle, 21st Infantry, Acting Field Quartermaster and C. S., and a guard of ten men will remain at this camp in charge of the temporary field depot until further orders.

XIII. Lieut. John Q. Adams, 1st Cavalry, A. A. A. G., District of the Lakes, and commanding detachment "H," troop 1st Cavalry, will furnish from his command such details as may be required for the Howitzer Battery, and accompany the District Commander. Lieut. Adams will be prepared to communicate by signals with the Signal Sergeant who has been detailed for duty with the troops operating on the east side of the Modoc position.

XIV. Assistant Surgeon Henry McEldery, U. S. A., will give the necessary directions and instructions to the medical officers serving with the different commands and detachments in the field.

By order of
FRANK WHEATON,
Brevet Maj. Gen. U. S. Army, Lieut. Col. 21st Infantry,
Commanding District of the Lakes.

OFFICIAL—
JOHN Q. ADAMS,
1st Lieut. 1st Cavalry, A. A. A. Gen.

HEADQUARTERS CAVALRY COMMAND,
Clear Lake, Cal., June 4, 1873.

Brig. Gen. John E. Ross, O. V. M., in the Feild —

GENERAL: I am in receipt of your note of this instant at 10 o'clock A. M. The Department Commander is collecting all the Modoc captives at the island in Tule Lake, and it is requested that you send your captives to that point as early as possible, or if more convenient they can be sent to me at this place, if they are forwarded within the next two days. When the services of the two Modocs, Jim and Frank, are no longer required by you, let them come here.

I am, General, very respectfully,
Your Ob't servant,
JOHN GREEN,
Major 1st Cavalry, Commanding.

OFFICIAL COMMUNICATION

From the Governor of Oregon to the Secretary of the Interior, Relative to the Indian Title and Rights of Settlers in Wallowa Valley, Oregon.

STATE OF OREGON, EXECUTIVE OFFICE, }
Salem, July 21, 1873.

To Hon. Columbus Delano,
    Secretary of the Interior:

SIR:—I beg leave to call your attention to the very grave and important question now pending before your Department, touching the subject of vacating the Wallowa Valley, Union county, Oregon, for the purpose of securing the same to Joseph's band of Nez Perce Indians, and to submit the following views thereon for your consideration.

On and prior to the 11th day of June, 1855, the Nez Perce tribe of Indians occupied lands lying partly in Oregon and partly in Washington Territory, between the Cascade and Bitter Root Mountains. On said 11th day of June, 1855, the said tribe, by their chief, head men and delegates, numbering fifty-eight officials, made and concluded a treaty of peace and boundaries with the United States—Isaac I. Stephens acting on behalf of the United States for Washington Territory, and Joel Palmer for Oregon. By said treaty the Nez Perces ceded and relinquished to the United States all their right, title and interest in and to all territory before that time claimed and occupied by them, except a certain tract described therein, specifically reserved from the ceded lands as a general reservation for the use and occupancy of said tribe, and for friendly tribes and bands of Indians in Washington Territory. This general reservation embraced lands lying in part in Oregon, including Wallowa (Wolllow-how) Valley.

On the 9th day of June, 1864, a supplementary and amendatory treaty was concluded between the said Nez Perce tribe and the United States; the former being represented by fifty-one chiefs, head men and delegates, and the latter by Calvin H. Hale, Charles Hutchins and S. D. Howe, as Commissioners specially delegated.

By the latter treaty the Nez Perce tribe agreed to relinquish, and did relinquish to the United States all the lands reserved by the treaty of 1855, excepting a certain specified tract designated as "a home, and for the sole use and occupancy of said tribe." By this amendatory treaty the Nez Perce tribe relinquished to the United States all the territory embraced in the Reservation created by the treaty of 1855, which lay within the boundaries of the State of Oregon, including the said Wallowa Valley; so that on and after said 9th June, 1863, the Nez Perce tribe did not lawfully hold or occupy any lands within the State of Oregon. Joseph's band of Nez Perce Indians were in the treaty council of 1855, and Joseph signed the treaty. Their action recognized the tribal relations of their band, and bound all the persons and territory described therein. The Reservation named became the common property of the whole tribe. Joseph and his band acknowledged these conclusions also by accepting the benefits of the treaty of 1855. But Joseph refused to acknowledge the treaty of 1863, while a large majority of the chiefs and head men of the Nez Perce tribe signed the same. Joseph died in 1871, and his sons claim the land which was relinquished to the United States in 1863, including Wallowa Valley. This claim is based on the idea that the band which they represent was not bound by the treaty of 1863.

The United States had established the policy of treating with the Indians as tribes and nations. This policy was predicted on the necessary fact that organized action by the tribe or nation binds the whole body and all of its members. The treaty of 1855 is the organized action of the Nez Perce tribe, in relation to land in which the whole tribe had a common interest. If the Government shall admit that one sub-chief, out of more than fifty joined in council, can, by refusing his signature, or by absenting himself, defeat the operation of a treaty, the policy of making treaties would be valueless and but few treaties would be binding. For there exists hardly a treaty with Indians west of the Rocky Mountains in which all the sub-chiefs and head men joined, and against which they have not positively protested. If we draw our conclusions from the former practice of the Government, or from assimilated cases of foreign treaties, it must be admitted that the treaty of 1863 bound all the Nez Perces and extinguished the Indian title to all lands previously occupied by that tribe lying within the State of Oregon.

Acting upon this conclusion, by order of the General Land Office, bearing date May 28, 1867, the public lands in Wallowa Valley and vicinity were directed to be surveyed and opened for settlement. The surveys made under this order amounted to eleven townships, which were approved May 9, 1868. From time to time, since that period, citizens of this State have become settlers upon these lands to such an extent, as I am now informed, that eighty-seven farms have been located and pre-emption and homestead claims have been filed thereto in the U. S. Land Office at La Grande.

Upon this statement of facts I urge that the Indian title to the lands occupied by these settlers has been doubly extinguished. First by treaty, and second, by force of law. As the Indians have only a right of occupancy, and the United States have the legal title, subject to occupancy, and with an absolute and exclusive right to extinguish the Indian title of occupancy, either by purchase, conquest, or by legal enactment, it would follow that if the treaty of 1863 did not completely extinguish the Indian title to the lands in question, the acts of the Government in surveying the Wallowa Valley and opening the same for settlement and the consequent occupancy of the same by settlers under the provisions of the several acts of Congress affecting such lands, and the recognition of these claims by the Local Land Office of the United States, would work a complete extinguishment of the Indian title by operation of law, as far as the occupied lands are concerned.

There are other Chiefs and head men of the Nez Perces, who did not sign the treaty of 1863, and who have refused and still do refuse to acknowledge its binding force. If the Government shall in this instance accede to the demands of Joseph's band and create a new Reservation for them, or shall admit in their favor the nullity of the treaty of 1863, as far as they are concerned, a score of like demands from other discontented bands, connected with other neighboring tribes, living under treaties negotiated in a similar way, will be immediately pressed upon the attention of the Indian Bureau. I am thoroughly persuaded that if the proposed surrender of the Wallowa Valley, and the adjacent regions, to these Indians, be now consummated as demanded, the measure, if it works as a special pacification in this instance, will cause a general dissatisfaction, not only with the Nez Perces, but with all neighboring tribes living under treaty relations, and this character of work will have to be entered upon and carried out as to all.

The declaration made by Congress March 3d, 1871, that "hereafter no Indian nation or tribe within the territory of the United States shall be acknowledged or recognized as an independent nation, tribe, or power, with whom the United States may contract by treaty," appears to me to relieve the Department from entangling itself with an effort to reform past treaties, as such, and to leave the Indian Office unembarrassed to adopt such policy as will subserve the best interests of both whites and Indians, without submitting its judgment to the caprices of untutored savages.

In addition to what I have urged against re-establishing any part of the Nez Perce Indians in Oregon, on grounds growing out of this particular case, I would respectfully press upon your consideration the general policy of the Government heretofore steadily pursued, of removing as expeditiously as circumstances would permit of, all Indians from the confines of the new States, in order to give them the opportunity of early settlement and development and to make way for civilization. This State has already much of its best soil withheld from being occupied by an industrial population in favor of Indians.

The region of country in Eastern Oregon not now settled

and to which the Wallowa Valley is the key, is greater in area than the State of Massachusetts. If this section of our State, which is now occupied by enterprising white families, should be remanded to its aboriginal character, and the families should be removed to make roaming ground for nomadic savages, a very serious check will have been given to the growth of our frontier settlements, and to the spirit of our frontier people in their efforts to redeem the wilderness and make it fruitful of civilized life.

There is abundant room for Joseph's band on the present Nez Perce Reservation, and the tribe desire to have this band observe the treaty of 1863. I learn that young Joseph does not object to going on the Reservation at this time, but that certain leading spirits of his band do object, for the reason that by so doing they would have to abandon some of their nomadic habits and haunts. The very objection which they make is a strong reason why they should be required to do so; for no beneficial influence can be exerted by agents and missionaries among the Indians while they maintain their aboriginal habits. *Joseph's band do not desire Wallowa Valley for a Reservation and for a home.* I understand that they will not accept it on condition that they shall occupy it as such. The reason of this is obvious; they can have better land and a more congenial climate at a location which has been tendered them upon the Nez Perce Reservation. This small band wish the possession of this large section of Oregon simply for room to gratify a wild, roaming disposition, and not for a home.

There are but seventy-two warriors of this band. The white settlers in the Wallowa country number eighty-seven. There are also in the Wallowa Valley two incorporated companies, the Wallowa Road and Bridge Company and the Prairie Creek Ditch Company. The improvements of these settlers and companies have been assessed, as I am informed, by a commissioner appointed under the direction of your department, to the amount of $67,860.

Considering that the demands of Joseph's band were made during the period of the apparently successful resistance of the Modoc outlaws against the treaty stipulations with the Klamaths, and that now the Modocs are subdued, it will doubtless be much less expensive to the Government, and much more consistent with its general Indian policy, to induce Joseph's band by peaceable means to make their home on the Nez Perce Reservation, than to purchase the rights of white settlers now in the Wallowa Valley. The people of this State have uniformly recognized the boundaries of legally defined Indian Reservations, and have abstained from attempting to establish settlements thereon. In all instances of various difficulties between settlers and Indians on our frontier, since the Reservation system has been extended to Oregon, hostilities have resulted rather from Indians refusing to confine themselves to their treaty limits than from any attempt of the settlers to encroach upon Reservations. This was the case with the Yakimas in 1855, who killed three miners outside of their treaty limits, and then murdered Indian Agent Boland, who visited them to remonstrate against their perfidy. This was the case last autumn with the Modocs, and is now the case with Joseph's band, in the light in which the treaty of 1863 has heretofore been held by the General Government and by the people of Oregon.

I believe the facts will sustain me in saying that at all

times and under all circumstances our frontier settlers have been as well disposed toward the Indians, and as moderate and forbearing as those of any other frontier, and as much so as the people of any other State would be under like circumstances.'

Urgently pressing upon your careful consideration the peculiar features of this subject, and on behalf of the interests of this State and of the settlers in Wallowa Valley and vicinity, asking that the preliminary steps taken for the vacation of said Valley for the purpose of creating a Reservation for Indians may be rescinded,

I have the honor to be
Your ob't servant,
L. F. GROVER,
Governor of Oregon.

www.ingramcontent.com/pod-product-compliance
Lightning Source LLC
Chambersburg PA
CBHW022152090426
42742CB00010B/1485